EAST COAST RAMBLE

POEMS AND SHORT ESSAYS

S.A. BROWN

For Mum and Dad

Introduction

In April and May 2021 – as England slowly emerged from the stringent coronavirus restrictions – I travelled along a good stretch of her beguiling east coast.

I visited the Lincolnshire, Yorkshire and Northumberland coastlines (with a few forays inland) including: Skegness, Ingoldmells, Mablethorpe, Saltfleet, Lincoln, Cleethorpes, Grimsby, Hornsea, Skipsea, Bridlington, Beverley, Filey, Scarborough, Tynemouth, Whitley Bay, Blyth, Morpeth, Alnwick, Bamburgh and Berwick-upon-Tweed.

I found places instinctively eager to welcome visitors with open arms, but also reticent after over a year of relentless bad news and false hope. I found towns that were run-down and out-of-luck, but with inhabitants happier and friendlier than in the wealthiest of leafy suburbs.

I found seascapes of awe-inspiring beauty, and old buildings of quiet majesty, and ports and ships of great historical significance. And I found a people weary and weathered – but not beaten – by the weirdest year of their lives.

This is a small collection of poems and short essays inspired by this trip. It is something of a hotchpotch of a collection – not everything is directly about the east coast, but at the very least they are things I wrote, or thought about, whilst I was there. (For example, the poem 'On the Edges' was originally written for my *Somewhere or Anywhere?* collection, but I thought it would fit nicely here too.)

I hope it can provide a little snapshot of a very curious period in English life.

S.A. Brown

Poems

Short Essays

Ramble Tamble

Ramble Tamble – CCR on blast,
Seeking refuge from the future and past,
Immersing in the present, as each second ticks by,
The easiest company: just me, myself and I.

A rooftop pint just gets me thinking,
As we emerge from the abyss, pale and blinking,
Locked Out; Locked In; Locked Up; Locked Down,
First glimpses of life in this honest English town.

A load of lads nearby – a rowdy rabble,
And behind all the bluster and babble,
Are sharp streetwise smarts,
As we talk about life in these forgotten parts.

The sun gives a full-frontal flirt,
The waitress smokes and smoulders, prime and pert,
With hypnotic hips (if only she was single),
Candy floss, doughnuts, a distant funfair jingle.

A rooftop haven in a straightforward place,
They look you in your eye and tell you to your face,
A little pocket of life as 'normality' restarts,
The beers keep coming till the sun departs.

Frank Sinatra sings us farewell,
As I put down my glass and try not to dwell,
On the melancholy of England on an April night,
And the waitress's glance as I slip out of sight.

Keep Going

*'With all its sham, drudgery and broken dreams, it is still a
beautiful world.'* Max Ehrmann, *Desiderata*

When the burdens seem too much to bear,
When the light burns from the spotlight glare,
When there's scarcely a second to stand and stare,
Keep Going.

When world events leave you lost and spinning,
When you find yourself knocked back to the beginning,
When you're sick of the blather, the lies and the sinning,
Keep Going.

When the smug politician smirks and spouts,
When the newshounds stick in their snouts,
When the windbag witters and the show-off shouts,
Keep Going.

When a dream dies or a loved one passes,
When you sail away and adrift from the masses,
When the ground underfoot fills with cracks and
crevasses,
Keep Going.

When the downbound train reaches its slope,
When the tether is touched at the end of the rope,
When the hardest word to conceive is 'hope',
Keep Going.

Keep Going, Keep Going, Keep Going.

And therein lies the trick,
As if with a thumb-click,
Or a wand-flick,
Even the sternest sceptic,
Will soon jump into a heel-kick,
If you just Keep Going.

Author's Note: Though I have personally been fortunate and in good spirits throughout the last year, this poem was written in response to news reports that the lockdown was (unsurprisingly) having a detrimental effect on the lives and health of many.

A Shoplifter in Grimsby

It's a bright Friday morning, 11:53,
In the sun-bathed centre of Grimsby,
When a man, shrouded in mask and hoodie,
Sticks two fingers up to society.

He strides straight up to the budget store,
Through its automatic glass door,
Past the row upon row of frozen galore,
Like a stricken ship seeking shore.

He reaches the booze aisle, scans left and right,
Hoping to sneak in and out of sight,
Downtrodden and drowning, at the depth of his plight,
Worn and weary and sick of the fight.

He grabs a bottle of liquor – dark and alluring,
Heart pumping and brain whirring,
The rights and wrongs of the law blurring,
A shop employee staring and stirring.

He feigns relaxation, has a marauding stroll,
Nearly lets out a whistle – such an easygoing soul,
As innocent as a newborn foal,
But each nervy minute is a mounting drum roll.

The crescendo crashes, and the shoplifter has bolted,
Just for a second, the staff member faltered,
He weighs up his options – is it worth being assaulted?
Can this desperate down-and-out be halted?

The shoplifter scrambles to the cobbled street,
Proud of his carefully-executed feat,
The taste of freedom and liquor so sweet,
Marching to his own lawless beat.

But it's half a job – he hasn't run far enough,
The employee emerges, grabs his scruff,
He has a scowl and buzz cut, and looks pretty tough,
He decided to call the shoplifter's bluff.

An everyday hero, who risked his neck,
He'd be the last to leave a sinking shipwreck,
Going way above his generic job spec,
And far beyond his miserly pay cheque.

But back to the shoplifter. What compels a man to steal?
How must the desperation feel?
He should be punished. Should he be pitied as well?
As midday is marked by the chiming church bell.

Author's Note: I did actually witness something like this happen in Grimsby, though some of the finer details are the product of artistic licence.

McDystopia

I'd been on the road all morning and needed a bite to eat. I was a few miles inland from the Northumberland coast, and my options were limited. Rain was lashing down with thunderous force. Inevitably, inexorably, the famous Golden Arches loomed into view.

It would do a job, I reasoned. Thirty-seven years after his death, Ray Kroc is still luring us in with the timeless combination of speed, affordability and familiarity. (The excellent film *The Founder*, with Michael Keaton playing Kroc, charts his ruthless and ingenious success in transforming McDonald's from a small-town mom-and-pop burger joint into a global phenomenon.)

I rounded the corner for the drive-thru, only to be met with the longest queue of cars I had ever seen outside a food establishment. It stretched for hundreds of yards. It was a comical sight, as people sat patiently, drumming their dashboards, playing with their hair, or fiddling on their phones, waiting for the queue to edge forward a few inches at a time. It was like rush hour in Los Angeles.

McDonald's are damn efficient, but they aren't *that* damn efficient. The queuing customers would be waiting for ages. They're probably the same people who get up at 5am for the Boxing Day sales, lining up outside DFS. Perhaps the waiting is part of the thrill. Each to their own.

I hoped that actually going inside and ordering in person would speed things up (this was just about allowed under the coronavirus restrictions) so I pulled into the car park. It was still raining heavily, and I spotted a small line of people huddled pathetically outside the entrance. I joined them, resigned to my fate, not even bothering to hunch my shoulders to alleviate the drenching.

One of the most amusing (or, perhaps, darkly amusing) side effects of the pandemic has been the emergence of newly-anointed bouncers outside supermarkets, shops and cafés. A job is a job, and all that, and I'd never begrudge anybody their work. But many of them seem to enjoy the little power that has come their way: *Wait there, sir. One in, one out, madam. Please queue in an orderly fashion. Sanitise your hands, and remember your masks!*

This employee-turned-bouncer summoned us in slowly from the downpour, one by one, when he saw fit. In the ten minutes I was queuing outside, a slew of Just Eat and Deliveroo drivers whizzed back and forth with their bounties – there were clearly hundreds more customers, sat at home, eager for their late-morning fix.

Eventually, I got the nod to go inside. (He may as well have unclipped a velvet rope.) I made my order on the futuristic touchscreen and took my receipt, before being pointed to a designated waiting area.

There were countless signs and exhortations on the floors and on the walls. *Stand here! Wait here! Keep your distance! Hands, face, space!* It's a miracle we can all remember how to breathe, without being constantly told to inhale and exhale.

The employees behind the counter worked tirelessly; the orders never stopped for a second. Most of them looked young, around college/university age, and they kept everything ticking over with metronomic care.

But, despite my admiration for the work ethic of the staff, the whole scene gave me the creeps. Everybody waited obediently in their little spot – their eyes poking out from above their de-humanising masks – not daring to converse, or move, or risk the wrath of the eagle-eyed bouncer, or the several other staff members wearing high-vis jackets. We're all so used to it now.

I couldn't help but wonder how small businesses are supposed to compete with these militant corporations. Small pubs and restaurants, without outside seating, are not allowed to serve food until 17 May. McDonald's, meanwhile, are evidently making a killing. They had people flocking from miles around.

And why are fast-food joints benefiting when the first line of defence against the coronavirus is good health and fitness? It's all so muddled, but we all have to shuffle into line – supine and obedient – and pray that our freedoms will eventually be handed back to us (a blatant contradiction in terms).

A little boy waited patiently with his dad. How much longer does this need to go on before he begins to think this is normal? I spoke to a teacher recently whose class of five-year-olds don't know how to play outside properly, as they've been so conditioned to stay in their designated areas (marked with cones). For their whole school lives they've been told not to mix with their peers in other classes.

The social, educational and economic consequences of this lockdown will be felt for decades to come.

As I drove away, I reflected (as I often have in the last year) on the famous Benjamin Franklin quote: 'Those who would give up essential Liberty, to purchase a little temporary Safety, deserve neither Liberty nor Safety.'

As so often with this type of pithy quotation, the context is lacking. Mr Franklin was referring to a tax dispute between the Pennsylvania General Assembly and the Penn family, and it can be unwise to apply an out-of-context remark from the eighteenth century to our present predicament.

Nonetheless, I think it neatly captures the great dichotomy and power struggle at the heart of western civilisation: Liberty versus (so-called) Safety. We have all witnessed and experienced an extraordinary shift in the relationship between the government and its electors throughout the pandemic.

So much so that a trivial food stop at McDonald's can serve as a microcosm of our Brave New World: a society governed by bossy officialdom, illogicality and state-sponsored panic and fear, illustrating (as we have so often seen throughout history) the terrifying conformity of human beings, particularly when their conformity is regarded as a moral virtue.

On the Edges

Time wind-sweeps by, coastlines erode,
In seaside towns, where progress has slowed.
The mocking splendour of a grand hotel,
Where ghosts wander and dreams dwell.

Victorian shadows and silhouettes,
Weathered donkeys and sudden sea frets.
Church peaks and dark-stained bricks,
On the fringes of our island politics.

Rusty coppers for merry arcade thrills,
Like Edwardians on their break from the mills.
'Wake weeks' – the town would titter and teem,
Top hats and trams, an idyllic English dream.

A seagull squawks, surveys and swoops,
A Union Jack on the pier fades and droops.
E-cigarettes, gold pawnbrokers, boarded-up windows,
Hope is hard to find where the sea wind blows.

It was a hotspot for honeymoon delight,
A fortress for our naval might.
The townspeople are the sea-salt of the earth,
Enriched by ocean air from birth.

But they live in the shadow of what came before,
They live on the edges, and they deserve more.

Life in the Lay-By

Neither coming nor going,
Neither going nor coming.
Just sat in the lay-by,
Tunelessly humming.

To the generic radio beat,
Monotonously thumping.
As our backs start to ache,
From the front-seat slumping.

Dull and drab,
No wind, rain or sun.
No journey, no destination,
No follies, no fun.

No location in sight,
Betwixt and between.
Steam from the burger van,
Clouding the windscreen.

A seized-up engine,
Cold and still.
From prolonged inaction,
And lack of thrill.

Gearstick in neutral,
Handbrake firmly on.
How many delays does it take,
For all hope to be gone?

The litter-strewn tarmac,
The axle-breaking potholes.
The flickering street light,
The transient souls.

It's life in the lay-by,
We've patiently sat through.
It's time to get back on the road,
And leave it all in our rear-view.

The Collingwood Touch

Son of a trader on the banks of the Tyne,
No silver spoon or noble bloodline,
Rose through the ranks to defend our coastline,
Like some hearty *Boys' Own* storyline.

Thirteen when he first left land to serve,
An honest young man, keen to observe,
Sharp of mind and steady of nerve,
Destined to scale an upward curve.

The vast, open seas were his domain,
Across the Atlantic, and back again,
Wherever the Royal Navy would deign,
To fight or flex its next campaign.

With his faithful dog by his side,
He navigated the chopping tide,
Caribbean to Cadiz – truly worldwide,
Running his ship with precision and pride.

Eagle-eyed, attentive and fair,
He treated all his men with care,
No need for flogging, just a stern glare,
Their loyalty followed him anywhere.

It wasn't all a smooth sail,
There was many a headwind gale,
Many an enemy plotting him to fail,
And many an effort to no avail.

But he stayed stoic and true,
At Trafalgar he fronted the queue,
Leading his ship of the bravest few,
A talisman and his well-drilled crew.

Nelson passed and a nation wept,
Into his shoes his good friend stepped,
His eye on his telescope, his hair windswept,
He rarely rested and scarcely slept.

He could seldom enjoy his Morpeth bliss,
A distant memory of a parting kiss,
As his body aged he would reminisce,
Of all his daughters' days he'd had to miss.

For his duty, he sacrificed all,
He fearlessly answered his country's call,
He gave his life to prevent her fall,
He lies forever with Nelson and St. Paul.

Devoted to all that was true and right,
The Collingwood touch was firm yet light.

*Author's Note: This poem was inspired by my visit to Admiral
Collingwood's monument in Tynemouth.*

Football and Globalisation

One of the biggest news stories during my travels was about the future of English football. The so-called 'Big Six' (which, for some reason, included Spurs) planned a dramatic departure to a European Super League, along with some of the continent's heavyweight clubs.

The reaction was febrile and furious, and the match between Liverpool and Manchester United was postponed as a result of fan protests. Generally, I sympathise with the fans who are outraged at such a shameless money-grab, but I also think it's bizarre that they seem so surprised and offended – the ESL is the logical extension of English football's long-standing and well-documented relationship with greed. It's the rational next step.

The 'death' of English domestic football occurred many years ago. One could cite the formation of the Premier League in 1992 as the turning point, or perhaps Roman Abramovich's takeover of Chelsea in 2003. Either way, the horse hasn't just bolted – it's a good ten furlongs around the track. To use another metaphor, it's like grieving over a body which was buried about twenty years ago.

For many years, the Premier League has been a ruthless plutocracy, and the top clubs are now the playthings of billionaires. Ultimately, they are at the top because they can spend more than their rivals.

Corporations compete with desperation for the TV rights (again, worth billions) and the concerns of the everyday, English fans are as low on the list of priorities as they could be. Kick-off times, ticket prices, short-termism from owners; these are just some of the areas in which the fans are treated with contempt.

It's a hyper-global, multi-national competition that just happens to be situated geographically in England. The 1996 FA Cup Final, between Liverpool and Manchester United, featured only two players in either squad from outside Britain and Ireland: Peter Schmeichel and Eric Cantona (who are, incidentally, two of the greatest players in Premier League history). The 2019 FA Cup final, between Manchester City and Watford, included seventeen players from outside Britain and Ireland in the starting line-ups alone.

The arrival of spectacular foreign stars in the 1990s – Bergkamp, Ginola, Klinsmann, Zola and, of course, Cantona and Schmeichel – was a wonderful thing for the game, but it quickly heralded a monumental shift. Mediocre foreign players began clogging up every squad, and the number of English players has hovered between 30 and 40 per cent in recent years (a lower native contingent than all other major European leagues). It has improved slightly in the last few seasons, since the nadir of 24 per cent one weekend in the winter of 2018, which forced even the mild-mannered Gareth Southgate to complain about the lack of opportunities for young English players.

It's not xenophobic to ask if the pendulum has swung too far the other way, and to wonder exactly who is benefiting from this rapid globalisation. Some would argue the English fans are benefiting from higher standards, and from watching the 'best league in the world' – plus, the brightest young English players are being exposed to a higher calibre of player, which can only be a good thing. Talent doesn't care about passports, after all, and this essay is no argument for quotas or ring-fences.

I'm merely pointing out a *doublethink* which underlies (and undercuts) so much of the outrage over the plans for a European Super League. The Premier League is *not* for the English fans. It's *not* for the development of English players. It's certainly *not* for the national team, as illustrated by the overwhelming power the Premier League has in comparison to the FA.

It's a globalised playground for sheiks, oligarchs and magnates. Why, then, are fans so determined for the 'integrity' of the domestic structure to remain in place? And why do they act with such surprise and outrage to a move which is perfectly logical considering the trajectory of the last three decades?

Such shock is many, many years too late. Every time a working-class English fan buys a ticket to the Emirates stadium, or buys a replica shirt with 'Etihad' emblazoned on the front, they are contributing to their own marginalisation. They are digging their own graves.

The footballer-turned-boxer Curtis Woodhouse summed it up perfectly, when he tweeted:

> *Makes me chuckle the outrage about the European super league stuff... the English premier league was built on sheer greed! Every team in it bludgeoned their way to the top table by spending big money and now they want more!!! You reap what you sow guys.*

He added:

> *I don't care either way. The days of my enjoying Premier League football went years ago. I'd rather watch Bridlington Town vs North Ferriby with my two sons, have a beer and a burger then chat with the supporters and players in the bar at full time. That's football for me.*

I wholeheartedly agree. I also gave up on Premier League football many years ago, even after working as a journalist with the privilege of watching games from the press box. I'd rather spend my time watching a game in the Northern League, which I played in as a teenager, or just doing something else.

The players' mawkish PR messages on social media; the cowardly diving and play-acting; the political virtue-signalling; the modern superclubs cynically cashing in on their heritage and tradition when they bear no resemblance to their forbearers – it all just leaves me cold.

Manchester City's dominance is simultaneously spellbinding and utterly boring. Pep Guardiola has spent over £400 million on defenders alone, and a City 'B' team would be pushing for a top-four finish. When Manchester United and Arsenal dominated in the '90s and early 2000s, they could still get turned over away at Coventry or Middlesbrough or Southampton, and from 1996/97 to 1998/99 the league was won with 75, 78 and 79 points respectively (not the 100 that City and Liverpool have pushed in recent seasons).

There were always richer clubs and (relatively) poorer clubs, but the gulf is now astonishing. Manchester City play exquisite football – on their day they look untouchable – but so they should. They're operating in a different stratosphere to a Burnley or a Sheffield United. Is it really so absurd that their regular opponents should be Barcelona rather than Brentford?

I find it impossible to *care* anymore, even if there will always be a residual interest because of my childhood love of the game. It's not my place to tell other people to stop caring – any football fan is entitled to think whatever they want – and part of me admires those who earned a temporary reprieve with their protests. But it's a Pyrrhic victory at best.

Whether teams play in the 'English' Premier League or the European Super League is not an important distinction for me. That battle was lost long ago.

Good luck to the 'Big Six'. My only suggestion is that each club should rename themselves before making the leap to the ESL – they should all get big corporate sponsors on board and become franchises. Coca-Cola Chelsea, Microsoft Man City, Amazon Arsenal. Why not? At least it would be honest.

*

The forces of globalisation, and the resultant left-behinds, were constantly on my mind during my trip along the east coast. It seemed appropriate, therefore, that the ESL story dominated the news cycle for a few days whilst I was there.

I walked past Blundell Park – a proper old-school ground on the edge of The Humber – and the largesse of the Premier League can leave a sour taste when compared with the financial struggles of clubs like Grimsby Town (who have been relegated from the Football League).

The coronavirus restrictions could prove to be the fatal blow for many lower-league and non-league clubs, who could very easily go the way of Bury FC in the next few years.

Why does this matter? What God-given right do football clubs have to survive when *all* businesses have been affected by globalisation (and, now, the ramifications of lockdown)? Why are they so special?

Whether you value football or not, it's clear that the decline of these proud, historic entities – rooted deeply in the folklore and identity of the communities around them – is part of a broader pattern of neglect and under-investment in areas of the country that have seen better days. This problem isn't restricted to coastal areas, of course, but it is especially evident in seaside towns.

And as many lower-league clubs face existential crises on a monthly basis, the powers that be at the top of English football plot their way to greater riches. They, quite literally, want to leave domestic English football behind. It's perfectly symbolic. Again, good luck to them.

But spare me the sanctimony next time I'm supposed to be 'inspired' by football's political gestures, or when the same chairmen, directors and dignitaries enjoy the World Cup in Qatar in 2022 – where the games will be played in stadiums built by modern slaves.

Decisions, Decisions

'We don't know a millionth of one per cent about anything.'
Thomas Edison

Every serendipitous second is a sliding door,
> A hair's breadth can separate peace from war.
The best-laid plans beg to be wrecked,
> Yet we cannot quarrel or object.
Just follow Kipling's timeless rules,
> And stoop and build with worn-out tools.

Only so much can be controlled,
> Life cannot be tricked or cajoled.
On ifs and buts we cannot dwell,
> The future we cannot foretell.
And the past can be a prison cell,
> Where nobody can hear you yell.

So next time you're in a pickle,
> Remember fate is fleeting and fickle,
As we struggle to understand a jot,
> Of what on earth occurs on this
Beautiful, beguiling, maddening
> Pale Blue Dot.

An A to Z of the English East Coast

A is for Ambling cliffside,
B is for Battered and fried,
C is for Calming tide.
D is for Dogs everywhere,
E is for Easeful deck chair,
F is for Fresh sea air.
G is for Greasy spoon,
H is for Hazy afternoon,
I is for Inexpensive honeymoon.
J is for Jolly foray,
K is for Kebab takeaway,
L is for Long summer day.
M is for Mobile RV,
N is for Nautical history,
O is for Old quay.
P is for Poignant memorial,
Q is for Quiet lull,
R is for Ruthless seagull.
S is for Sand train,
T is for Torrential rain,
U is for Umbrella in vain.
V is for Vikings long ago,
W is for Wistful and slow,
X is for Xmas in the snow.
Y is for Yearly returnees,
And Z is for Zero pomposities.

A Sense of Place (Bull Mountain: A Book Review)

Bull Mountain, by Brian Panowich (G.P. Putnam's Sons, 2015).

Sometimes, we remember the context of where and when we read a book, as much as the story itself. It is a magical element of reading; no book is ever read in the same way by two people. It's one of the few intensely personal endeavours left.

The very best books, of course, can transport the reader *beyond* their current surroundings. *Bull Mountain*, by Brian Panowich, is most definitely in that hallowed category. It creates an authentic and dynamic sense of place as well as any novel I have read.

I read the book in just a few sittings, often as rain was hammering on the roof of the caravan/mobile home I was staying in. They were peak reading conditions, and *Bull Mountain* transported me from the windswept east coast of England to the American South: the swampy, dark waters of the Bayou; the backwoods, the forests and the mountains; the moonshine, the pot, the meth and the lawlessness that pervade swathes of this vast and beautiful region.

And at the heart of it all was an epic family struggle, mapped out over decades and culminating in a brother versus brother confrontation, written so deftly as to subvert and surpass any clichés of the genre.

The story follows the Burroughs family through multiple generations. They have made their home on Bull Mountain, in North Georgia, and they are a law unto themselves. From their deep-rooted enclave, they transport alcohol and drugs with impunity.

We are introduced to Clayton Burroughs, who has tried his best to distance himself from his family of outlaws. He works as a sheriff in a neighbouring community, but he gradually and inevitably gets drawn into his family's business (and his past) when a federal agent arrives with a masterplan to bring the Burroughs down. The story encompasses loyalty, enmity, love, betrayal, revenge and everything in between.

It's raw, gritty and visceral. The setting reminded me of the first series of *True Detective*, pound-for-pound the greatest season of television I have seen, in which Matthew McConaughey's character (the detective Rust Cohle) explores the evil underbelly of deepest Louisiana. 'I get a bad taste in my mouth out here,' he says. 'Aluminium, ash. Like you can smell the psychosphere.'

In much the same way, you quickly sense and feel (and can almost taste and smell) the unique air and atmosphere of Bull Mountain. The location is essentially a character itself, which is something Panowich deliberately aimed for. He said: 'It was important to me that the mountain, as well as the hill country of North Georgia, be just as prominent and important to the story as the human characters.'

Panowich wrote the book whilst working as a firefighter in Georgia, and his familiarity with the area shines through. I doubt this could be written by a fleeting visitor to the region. Remarkably, it's his debut novel, and I will certainly be reading the sequel *Like Lions*.

I'll refrain from any spoilers, but I will say there's an impressively unpredictable twist towards the end. It was the perfect way to spend a rainy day or two, and I would highly recommend *Bull Mountain* to everyone, particularly those who enjoy what one critic called 'heartland noir' dramas.

And it will appeal to those who enjoy books written by real people who have lived real lives, far from the metropolitan chattering classes and their literati dinner parties.

The Joy of Silence

'Silence is the perfectest herald of joy.'
William Shakespeare, *Much Ado About Nothing*

In a noisy world, silence is the sweetest sound,
So rare and relaxing, so pure and profound.

Rush and haste and hassle create relentless din,
The only balm is silence, to look deep within.

To sit and ponder nothing, like Otis on his dock,
The ocean's lapping tides serving as the clock.

From morning sun to evening shadow,
Let your senses and spirit adapt to nature's flow.

And let the only soundtrack be the birds singing,
Instead of gripe, gossip and emails endlessly pinging.

Tune out the nonsense, lend an ear to the serene,
Give your tense temperament a full-service clean.

Life's incessant demands make it hard to achieve,
But try to give your brain a cleansing reprieve.

Revel in silence, time passes gently by,
Existing – no need to explain or justify.

Printed in Great Britain
by Amazon